Not Akhmatova

Poems and Adaptations

Noah Berlatsky

Ben Yehuda Press
Teaneck, New Jersey

Published by Ben Yehuda Press
122 Ayers Court #1B
Teaneck, NJ 07666

http://www.BenYehudaPress.com

To subscribe to our monthly book club and support independent Jewish publishing, visit https://www.patreon.com/BenYehudaPress

Jewish Poetry Project #40   **http://jpoetry.us**

ISBN13 978-1-963475-29-6 pb 978-978-1-963475-30-2 epub

Cover photo: Alphonse Maria Mucha, Photographs from the Study Trip to Russia Used for the Painting,"The Abolition of Serfdom in Russia," (1914), from the "Epic of the Slavs Cycle, Moscow," courtesy of the Getty Museum: https://www.getty.edu/art/collection/object/109EHW

Library of Congress Cataloging-in-Publication Data

Names: Berlatsky, Noah, author.
Title: Not Akhmatova : poems and adaptations / Noah Berlatsky.
Description: Teaneck, New Jersey : Ben Yehuda Press, 2024. | Series: The Jewish poetry project ; #40 | Summary:""Not Akhmatova" is a collection of poems that engage in dialogue with the work of Russian poet Anna Akhmatova, exploring themes of diaspora, identity, and language through adaptation and response. The book blends translation with original poetry to reflect on the intersections of personal and historical narratives within the Jewish and broader human experience"-- Provided by publisher.
Identifiers: LCCN 2024013488 (print) | LCCN 2024013489 (ebook) | ISBN 9781963475296 (paperback) | ISBN 9781963475302 (epub)
Subjects: LCGFT: Poetry.
Classification: LCC PS3602.E7576 N68 2024 (print) | LCC PS3602.E7576 (ebook) | DDC 811/.6--dc23/eng/20240329
LC record available at https://lccn.loc.gov/2024013488
LC ebook record available at https://lccn.loc.gov/2024013489

24 25 26 / 10 9 8 7 6 5 4 3 2 1   20240517

Contents

Introduction / ix

Introduction

The poems in *Not Akhmatova* are all inspired, or in conversation with, the work of Russian poet Anna Akhmatova (1889-1966). At the beginning of the 20th century, while Akhmatova was growing up, my own great-grandparents were emigrating from Russia to the United States to escape the things that most Jewish people in that part of the world were trying to escape. The experiences of oppression and national identity Akhmatova faced variously parallel and contrast with those of my relatives, so she's a poet who feels like she belongs to me and like she doesn't, an ambivalence characteristic of diaspora.

Some of the poems here border on translation, though words and meanings are changed fairly freely at the best of times. Other pieces scramble further afield; some are based on her words or ideas, others respond to or argue with her, some are about her. You can go down a rabbit hole to separate out who is who, or let it remain somewhat mysterious; those are both valid approaches to diaspora and identity.

This is not a work of scholarship; even if I wanted to attempt such, I'm a monoglot who's had to lean on Google and hints from other translators. If you want a less deliberately idiosyncratic approach to Akhmatova, Ruverses.com has a great collection of her poetry in English translation online. D.M. Thomas' short volume of selected poems is a good place to start in print.

Why Akhmatova

She's so very much herself
and I am not.

Leave Your Russia Forever

Akhmatova believed you can only sustain your art in your
    native country.
Akhmatova believed you can only sustain your art in your
    native language.

She said the Revolution was a kind of suicide.
She said Russia was a harlot who did not know who was
    defiling her.

And she heard a voice saying leave your deaf and sinful land.
And she heard a voice saying leave your Russia forever.

The border will wash your self from your self.
The border will wash your name from your name.

You will be new and you will not know shame.
You will be new and the old defeat forgotten.

But she was indifferent and she was calm.
But she filled her ears with Russian and did not listen.

She remained sorrowful but unstained by exile.
She remained sorrowful but pure as her nation.

Anna, the border washed your tongue from our tongue.
Anna, the border is a voice that said our name.

Noah Berlatsky

The White Stone

One memory is drowned in me.
In a well, a stone, white.
I will not remove it from me.
It is joy. It is night.

It is all my eyes see.
It is all you can see in my eyes.
It's a mournful thought, a story
inside, where the stone lies.

The gods turn people into things
that can still feel and know.
You've become me. The well sings
with mute wonder. With sorrow.

Lot's Wife

The righteous man followed God's messenger,
huge and terrible, like a black mountain.
His great back to Lot's wife was sorrow and fear.
She longed to stop and see just once again

the white spires of her home, the place
in the square where she sang to her children.
The windows of the house where in joy and pain
she gave birth to her children.

And so she turned back, for one last sight.
Her eyes like those windows were empty.
Her body was a pillar of salt, bleached white.
Her feet were rooted in place, like a memory.

We aren't supposed to mourn her.
She's a fool, and so many others burned.
They say do not look towards her
who defied God, and turned.

                     Noah Berlatsky

Confession

He forgave my sins, then silence.
The lilac dusk fell on the flame.
The dark shawl fell on my senses
my head, my body, my shame.

The voice said, "Virgin! Rise up…"
The heart beats on, beats on.
Through the cloth, the touch
makes the sign of the thumb.

Confession

I didn't sin; he did not forgive.
The flame was not lust.
I had nothing to confess or give.
I was baptized in dust.

Noah Berlatsky

Over the Water

Little butcher's boy
the deck creaks.
Hell is a pond
deeper than Russia.
Someone falls in
to my reflection
speaking nonsense.
Bubeleh, bubeleh.

In Dreams

We're separated forever, you and I.
But don't cry.
Instead, come to me at night in sleep.
We'll be two mountains, peak to peak
yearning, never getting nearer.
I see you clearer
in this atmosphere of dream,
above the clouds.
Dawn is a cold, didactic shroud.

                    Noah Berlatsky

That Unity That Is Separation

Translation.
Poetry.
Exile.
Breath.

Communication.
Love.
Zoom chat.
Death.

Marrying a Home

Submit to you? I'm not insane!
I only submit to God. The Lord is One.
Not yours. Not pain.
I have married a prison.

I came to you myself.
You howled like a wind in December.
And in your howling, I heard myself.
Outside—darkness, a cracked number.

Like a bird cracked against the window,
the body filled with weather,
driven, bound, its selves its fetters.

Goodbye, love. I have left the bones of our home
spread across black waters.
You sheltered me, though it was not me, nor shelter.

Noah Berlatsky

White Dove

He was jealous and tender and jealous.
He loved me like the sun burns the earth.
My white dove sang of a time before us
so he murdered that white bird.

As the red sun set, he said, "Laugh, love—
rejoice, sing, and write poetry."
So I dug a grave for my white dove
by the well near the alder tree.

I promised him never to grieve
but my words and my heart turned to stone.
The well is cold; I can't seem to leave.
Her voice calls, sweet, sad, and alone.

Native Soil

We don't even write songs about her.
We don't plan to go to her as into some mud-fouled paradise.
We don't bend to kiss her.
When we taste her on our lips we spit.
When we crawl on her she crawls under our fingernails
and we curse her.
When we walk on her, ill and broken, we feel her coat our lungs
and we don't remember her.
We refuse.

She's the grime under our eyelids we won't bother to remove.
She's the soil from our parent's graves ground into the scabs on
    our knees.

But our ghosts still writhe in her mouth.
And so we say she is theirs.
We won't say she's ours.
But she is.

                              Noah Berlatsky

Requiem

Not mine.
Not me. Someone
else, with a different name
is suffering beside that wall.
Blind wall.

Instead of an Epitaph

Can you describe this?
The stupor, the cold, the gate.
I can, yes.

A woman with blue lips
did not know my name.
Can you describe this?

Each order is a kiss
and every love an iron grate.
I can, yes.

The faces are a list
that's never read. They wait.
Can you describe this?

Her eyes know nothing yet.
Knowledge is always late.
I can, yes.

They're all dead now. The mist
lies on them like a weight.
Can you describe this?
I can, yes.

					Noah Berlatsky

Blank Page

Poetry
pre Gutenberg
written down
and read
in Russian
into memory
the blank page
of the head.

Memory
pre memory
the pogrom
written out
of Russian
by another sea
the blank page
of the dead.

Amnesty
post silencing
forgiveness
from the words
in Russian
kept in sanctity
the blank page
never said.

I Can't Remember The Title

Marble cracks. Iron rusts.
Gold loses its shine.
All that is, is gone in time.
All that is, is lost.

Even sorrow dulls in season.
You try to hold it and it goes.
God is merciful and knows
God's word will be forgotten.

 Noah Berlatsky

Say Freedom

My great uncle was named for Eugene V. Debs
the great socialist hero who said
"If there is one soul in prison, I am not free."
He died before he had to see
or apologize for Stalin's regime.

We're only saved from hypocrisy
by the grace of God, who spoke out of the whirlwind
to sneer at Job's suffering.
Even the Lord above has prisoned souls
he frees, and those

he leaves where they have fallen.
Akhmatova said, "I agree to everything.
Dark will be light and beauty sin."
And someone said, "Never again."
Someone speaks, but the sky's a lid.

Words don't get into heaven.

Crucifix

Mary Magdalene sobbed.
Peter was stone.
No one dared look at Mary, alone.

 Noah Berlatsky

Crucifix

The bereft of God
in grief, in shame
looked for someone to blame.

Cinque

Pity
is disgusting.
But when you pity me
it's like the sun inside me. Dawn
breaks me.

Breaks me
like dawn. The sun
is crawling from my mouth.
I am transformed by some blank God's
pity.

Noah Berlatsky

Perfect Song

Woven in my dark braid
a gentle, silver strand
of torment. Voiceless nightingale,
I think you understand.

You hear the distant cry
shake the slender willow branch.
You tremble against the wrong sky
pierced by the wrong descant.

But remember perfect quiet.
No rivals, no alarm.
Remember opening your throat
in the poisonous joy of song.

I Hear the Orioles

I hear the orioles grieving
summer's lovely long descent.
The snake's hiss of the sickle is reaping.
The grain in the fields is bent.

The short skirts of the binders flutter
like wind-caught autumn leaves.
A blackbird lifts, and then another
two dark eyes above the sheaves.

I'm not waiting for your touch
as the long night settles in.
But come look where we were touched
by innocence, and sin.

     Noah Berlatsky

Imitation of Akhmatova's Imitation of Innokenty Annensky

Why did I bend down
the corner of this page?

Why does the book always open
to the same page?

Maybe the poem is ours together.
Maybe you just glanced at the page.

A Tear

after Akhmatova's translation of Victor Hugo

A tear always washes away something.
A tear brings comfort.
A tear always washes away something.
It washes away comfort.

Don't ask why, don't ask why.
Child, child, there is no why.
Only comfort and tears.
Only comfort and tears.

 Noah Berlatsky

Crossing

after Akhmatova's translation of Rabindranath Tagore

Two villages are separated by a river.
And everyone wants to cross over in a hurry.
This one leaves the home of their father.
This one returns, rushing to the ferry.

Epochs pass, kingdoms are trampled down.
As rain falls, the river foams and floods.
Thirsty for a new life, parched dreamers drown
in a bowl of nectar or a bowl of mud.

One village has a secret name it hides.
The other guesses at the syllables, the tone
and keeps its own name hidden. From this side
they look afar with longing. They look with longing home.

It Doesn't Matter

It doesn't matter where you're bored,
so I came here to do nothing.
The mill on the hilltop leans towards
the years, which say nothing.

The bee lazily drowns in pollen.
By the pond I call to the naiad.
The buzzing goes on and on.
The thing in the water is dead.

The deep pond has drained and is shallow,
clogged with a red-brown scum.
Above the aspen the moon hangs low.
Time hangs down, dumb.

Time comes to me in new clothes
that smell of damp and new birth.
These words aren't mine. I close.
I'm ready again to be earth.

 Noah Berlatsky

The Snake

In my room there waits
a snake the color of my skin.
It needs nothing and it waits,
cold and slow and thin.

In the evening when I write
it watches without blinking
as if to catch each thought I write.
Its tongue is red as drinking.

At night when I can't sleep
its lidless eyes are open wide.
And when I dream, like sleep
across my dreams it slides.

In the morning, like water
my pale thoughts will drip.
From my shoulder, like water
my ribbon, pale, slips.

Cuckoo

I asked the cuckoo
how long I had to live.
In the water I can see you
hair spreading like a sieve
through which reflections sift.
The cuckoo calls to me
or I call to it, adrift
in an eye that I can't see.

 Noah Berlatsky

Slander

Slander followed me everywhere.
It squatted, a black bug in my ear,
a cloak of black bugs
around my dreams, chittering.
No one likes bugs. Everyone is disgusted
or frightened. Even they don't know which.

I'm not afraid. I know in myself
there is a self that is righteous, and my dreams
under a dead sky, in a dead city
walk without remonstrance.

Things, in short, could be worse.

I know, though, that eventually I'll die,
and that slander will attend, tireless,
at my left hand which has turned to dust.
Friends will sing a requiem and in it will be woven
that other requiem, like a ghost.
No neighbor will look
into the eyes of a neighbor
without seeing it there. Every neighbor will look away
like a ghost.

I tell myself that no one sees you when you're gone, anyway.
So what does it matter if they see an emptiness instead?
And slander, like an echo, says that it too is content.

Not Akhmatova

Courage

It is not bitter to be homeless.

Well, I thought courage would be
a well to draw from, sitting on a dry rock
somewhere high up, the cold clear sky
cruel as rock. My courage
and me, leaning one on the other
like sky and rock.

Well. It's not like rock at all.
More like mud the heart gets stuck in
sucking like thirst at a well,
till you can't see the sky, or much but thirst.
It will drink you, it will eat you
there on the rock.

It doesn't lift you up.
It pins you where you fell.

     Noah Berlatsky

Akhmatova

after Osip Mandelstam

Sorrow flows like a shawl of stone.

Return and Return

I can weep solemnly. I can be bored.
Thank God there are no more bells to lose.
The souls of all my shrouds have flown to the ground.
Five years have passed in an echoing of song.

Thank God there are no more bells to lose.
A silver willow has died beside the water.
Five years have passed in an echoing of song.
My shadow returns, an exhausted topic.

A silver willow has died beside the water.
Its branches rest in a September sleep.
My shadow returns, an exhausted topic.
The lyres hang from the palace like sunlight.

Its branches rest in a September sleep.
I can weep solemnly. I can be bored.
The lyres hang from the palace like sunlight.
The souls of all my shrouds have flown to the ground.

     Noah Berlatsky

Don't Look For Joy

Don't look for joy to any earthly thing.
Don't be attached to your wife or to your wealth.
Take the bread from your child as it is crying.
Give the last crumb to someone else.

Submit like a slave to the enemy you hate.
Crawl on your belly and kiss the rod.
Call the wolf your brother, and the snake.
Expect nothing from your God.

The Last Toast

To God who will not save.

To God who will not save.

To God who will.

To God who will.

To God who will not.

To God who will not.

To God.

To God.

To God.

To God.

To God who will not save.

To God who will not.

To.

To.

To.

To.

To God who will not.

To God who.

 Noah Berlatsky

To God who.

To God who.

To God who.

To God who will not.

Will not.

Will not.

Will.

Will not.

Will.

Will not.

To God who will not.

Drink.

Drink to.

Drink to God.

Drink to God who.

Will not drink.

Drink to God who.

Drink to God who.

Will not drink.

Will not drink.

Will not drink.

Will not drink.

Will not save.

To God who will not save.

     Noah Berlatsky

Song Last

Light steps. The glove
should go on the right hand
but here it is on the left

so that I can't hold you.
There are not supposed to be this many steps.
There are not supposed to be this many autumns

without you. Trees I don't know
are changing into ones I do.
It is like a revelation

that we will not meet again. There is no house
no bedroom, no candle. Only
an indifferent song at last.

The Guest

The poem is recalcitrant.
It won't come into meaning.
And then once it's there
It won't come out again.

I asked him, "What do you want?"
He said, "To be damned with you."
The sentences grew gaunt
and slipped into what I knew.

To touch a petal is not just to touch a petal.
To look at a ring is to take a ring.
The blackbird is splayed in the iris
like a beetle in the word "amber".

It's not much in the way of hell.
It's not much in the way of romance.
My name has visited the wrong alphabet
and put its feet up, refusing nothing.

You Will Hear The Thunder

You will hear the thunder
but you won't remember me.

You'll think, "That isn't thunder."
No lightning struck; the air
did not expand.

There is nothing left behind to say
this was my hand.

Inspiration

I used to think that no one drew Superman in the comic-books. I thought they must have a kind of rubber-stamp of Superman. They must have a lot of these stamps, posed in different ways. One flying; one hitting Lex Luthor. And for each panel they'd find the stamp, and they'd thump it down where they needed it. And that was how pictures of Superman were made.

Who drew the stamp? I wasn't sure about that. Maybe there was a stamp that made the stamp? I just knew that I couldn't draw Superman, so it made sense that no one else could draw Superman either. Art is impossible. Or not impossible. It exists only as a copy via some semi-industrialized and anonymous process. It exists through miraculous reproduction, miraculously absent inspiration.

Akhmatova said she got her inspiration from the backpack of Likho—an old woman in black who embodies misfortune. You can pass her to others with a gift. I wrote this very quickly, like stamping a white page, so that I would miss her.

Exile

Wretched, always—that's the exile.
Imprisoned, doomed, tubercular.
The road away is black and ever blacker.
A meal with strangers tastes like bile.

The meal is bread unleavened.
The black road hides you in her hat.
Cough up blood and read it like a map.
Sometimes that's the home you're given.

The Muse

When I'm waiting for her at the laptop
I'm not for a moment distracted by twitter
or Youtube, or youth, or dreams of honor.
They're nothing when she talks.

And here she comes, her hand on mine
guiding or reprimanding, it's hard to know.
I ask, "Did you hold Akhmatova so?"
Her laugh is sweet, if not exactly kind.

 Noah Berlatsky

Love Song, Maybe to Anna

after Nikolay Gumilev

Like the wind of a contented land
lovers grouse.
Like ripe corn that bends
the heads of the stubborn bow.

In the desert an Arab sings,
"From my body they tore my soul."
Above the blue sea the Greek is groaning:
"Like a seagull you flew into my soul."

Who is not a slave to beauty?
A Greek woman lights a lamp at night.
An Arab woman in love roasts coffee
in the tent at first light.

Across the steppes, across the years
the broad miracle grows broader.
Can you hear it thrumming, dear,
in this song, like silt in water?

Love, your smile is summer
and your slender hands fall gently.
Your black hair drowns me with wonder
in two-thousand-year-old honey.

Insomnia

A snoring wife
a snoring dog
and through the fog
of not sleeping
the morning's writing
mutters
and gutters behind
some mind.
The laptop glows. Oh,
unsunlit
world that sits
still. Hello.

   Noah Berlatsky

Brave Kitty

Stupid cat, it's just an owl
embroidered on the sheet.
Don't leave my lap—don't yowl!
You'll scare the mice. Their feet
scratch and flicker on the stair.
The candle has gone out.
The owl is here. It's here.
I'm not afraid of it.

Pictures

When someone dies all their pictures change.
You can't recognize them. That eye, that nose.
It was like that, but not like that.
It is not the same as what I see when I dream.
In here they are the same.
Out there the image keeps changing.
I have seen it. I have spoken to the pictures about it.
They smile. They speak. They remonstrate.
But not like they used to.

Noah Berlatsky

Alone

They threw so many stones at me
that I can't even feel where they hit.
Broken eyes and broken bones may be
a trap of bone, or a blue-black tower that sits

within, among my thoughts like towers.
There is sunlight in there moving like a mind
across the rocks stacked by the builders,
who thanking, I make my own, and kind.

All that enters now is wind like breathing
and a dove that rustles when I turn my head
like a pencil scratching, a poem weaving
together stones and light and what is said

somewhere outside, light and calm as a kiss
on the unfinished page which we have finished.

How Do We Say Goodbye?

How do we say goodbye?
The night is coming in.
Your eye won't meet my eye.
You're silent. I'm your twin.

Somewhere people are married.
Here we walk and then we walk.
Somewhere people are buried.
We are interred in thought.

Hard-packed is winter's snow.
No foot can leave a mark.
The house of dream, we know,
is welcoming. And dark.

    Noah Berlatsky

Misfortune

The moon is nailed above the lake.
It gapes like an open window
in some house, where you know
something ugly has taken place.

The owner lies in his own blood.
Someone's run away with some lover.
A child can't be found. By the water
there's a lost shoe clogged with mud.

Someone else's disaster
shines cold and beautiful as the moon.
We will be home safe, soon.
An owl calls, and small creatures shiver.

America

America is not an old peasant killing its meat.
It's a merchant who consumes but stays skull thin.
It will take money. It will take land.
But mostly it wants a corpse to stand on
so its rags can rustle higher
like a flag in a quiet wind.
Someone must hold it up.
Someone must water its base with bone.

Noah Berlatsky

Our Century

Why has our century turned to shit?
Maybe because, anxious and grief-stricken,
it plunged into a black sore a single digit
which broke and healed nothing.

In the west the sun is doused.
Across the city the light dies.
A white hand marks a cross on each house.
And the ravens call. And the ravens fly.

Settling In

We hope they'll pass, both Plague and War,
as they unpack and change the drapes.
We hope time wears and they grow bored.
But they are time, and they can wait.

                    Noah Berlatsky

To The Twilight of Freedom

after Osip Mandelstam

Raise a glass to the twilight of freedom
as the ship of freedom sinks through murk.
Bloated fish glow, blind eyes on glory's sun.
Our nets are heavy, drawing in the dark.

Heave and sing to the end of endless song
and lungs all clotted with the glue of mud.
Above somewhere the sparrows chatter on,
clouds of bright thoughts, conscripted for the dead.

Our judges rise from water into earth—
Leviathan, voice whining through the wires.
In the deep there is no sound but dearth.
Burdens crack like canvas sails in the mire.

Heave and sing to a world that heavy turns,
a wheel of lead, water that parts like thought.
The birdless, fishless wake of heaven churns.
We set our broken nets and we are caught.

The Ring

I won't be a ring on his hand.
I won't be a jewel in his crown.
I won't be the truth in his mouth.
I'm the thorn, the tarnish, the lie.
I'm the pen that will gouge out his eye.

 Noah Berlatsky

Dancing

We're all greedy and on display.
We make each other miserable
like clouds, birds, flowers
hammered to the wall.

I breathe in black fumes
from your strange pipe.
My slim legs are smooth.
My skirt is tight.

There are no windows.
No rain. We are trapped.
Your eyes are not closed.
They crawl like a cautious cat.

I want something.
Maybe to die in a while.
Some woman is dancing
who soon will be in hell.

Three Autumns

My understanding is that there are three autumns.

The first is not so bad. Children and lamp posts change color.
Trees gather acorns and the world scuttles off to a nest
of dappled light and breathing that shakes the caves
where they hide red moons and pocket change.

Executive wardrobes are renewed for another season.
It's a time of transformation and economic stimulus.
It is a great bronze horse born out of mulch.

And then the second autumn is death.

And the third?

I don't know.

 Noah Berlatsky

Not Like A River

Like a river I have stepped out of my life
into an alternate marvel universe multiverse
where all the metaphors are broken and the language flows
into the wrong grave.
I could have seen a different skyline
made out of different friends
casting shadows against the dawn of a different internet.
I don't even know whose poems I am writing.
I don't know whose poop is coming out of me.
I don't know if I would have found that funny
if I read my life in the original
rather than copying this other one
in hoofprints across Europe
leading into a mass of hoofprints
where my name wouldn't be and isn't.
Sometimes though you read a mirror
or look into a poem
and you see that echo pulling off its glasses like Clark Kent
or scribbling L'chaim on the golem's forehead.
Its eyes open and its big clay hands draw me
into that non-existent existence.
In such a year such a year
I would have been hauling a barge across a haddock
I would have been stapled to the ceiling of a salon dripping wit
I would be eyebrows and a nose
fluttering like a moth in the dark
envious of the lamp on the other side of the window
smearing its own destiny on the wall
like it's trying to invent television.
And on every channel is *Casablanca*
starring Ugarte who is not Ugarte
wheedling into the narrative that should be
about more important people.
I would despise you if I thought about you.
What right do I have to think?

Diaspora (Poem Without The Right Language)

pArt
thirteeN
laughiNg
dAwn
juAn flocK tHe froM A Tower lOok eVerything sAying

Again
loNg
beiNg
bAptized
And darK Have i'M drAft Through snOwflake relatiVes seA

grAveyard
aNd
iN
foAm
mArche King tHe coMe yeAr The lOrd's conVersation All

Are
doesN't
aNxiety
stAnd
shAdow masKs tHe soMe A Tympanum gOat-leg eVerything
  cleAr

   Noah Berlatsky

Anna Akhmatova

Anna Andreyevna Gorenko
Anna Akhmatova
Anna Gumilev
Anna Akhmatova
Anna Shileyko
Anna Akhmatova
Anna Punin
Anna Akhmatova
Anna Andreyevna Gorenko
Anna Akhmatova

To My Poems

To be fair, you didn't promise a whole lot.
The woods you led me to were mostly shrubs.
Your explosions fizzled out like thoughts.
Your thoughts wore down like pencil stubs.

A deeper muse might taste more bitter,
but who looks for consolation in a spill?
Small gifts, small expectations. Better
to know your art has not, and never will.

          Noah Berlatsky

Translation

Every rhyme
takes you somewhere else.

Translation

Each time
it's someone else.

62

Noah Berlatsky

To Anna Not To Anna

I just learned that my grandmother spoke Russian
like her ancestors who spoke Russian
when they did not speak something else.
Russians gave them orders
till they left the language lying behind
like blood on the snow shaking its fists.

I don't pick up anything that is mine because
nothing that drops on the earth like rainwater
is mine if it fills up the hollows.
It is only the water that runs off the earth
speaking its own language like frogs in the water
croaking in trees and on the horizon.

We left and we didn't take anything with us
and now the homelessness you gave us is ours
which includes the beauty and misery
pooling in the hollows. It includes the language taken
from my tongue which speaks now
for you, not for you, for the fish in the trees
who own the world that they're no part of.

Acknowledgements

"Lot's Wife" first appeared in *Cincinnati Review*

"To The Twilight of Freedom" was first published in *Synchronized Chaos.*

"Settling In" first appeared in *Asses of Parnassus*

Thanks to Bert Stabler, Orion Kidder, Elizabeth McClellan, and my wife and daughter for reading and providing feedback on parts of this manuscript. And thanks to Larry Yudelson and Julia Knobloch at Ben Yehuda Press for turning it into this book.

About the Author

Noah Berlatsky is a freelance writer from Chicago. He has published poetry chapbooks from above/ground press, Origami Poetry Project, LJMcD Communications, and has a collection forthcoming from Red Ogre. He is also the author of *Wonder Woman: Bondage and Feminism in the Marston/Peter Comics, 1941-48* from Rutgers UP.

The Jewish Poetry Project

jpoetry.us

Ben Yehuda Press

From the Coffee House of Jewish Dreamers:
Poems of Wonder and Wandering and the
Weekly Torah Portion by Isidore Century

"Isidore Century is a wonderful poet. His poems are funny,
deeply observed, without pretension." – *The Jewish Week*

The House at the Center of the World: Poetic
Midrash on Sacred Space by Abe Mezrich

"Direct and accessible, Mezrich's midrashic poems often tease
profound meaning out of his chosen Torah texts. These poems
remind us that our Creator is forgiving, that the spiritual and
physical can inform one another, and that the supernatural can
be carried into the everyday."
—Yehoshua November, author of *God's Optimism*

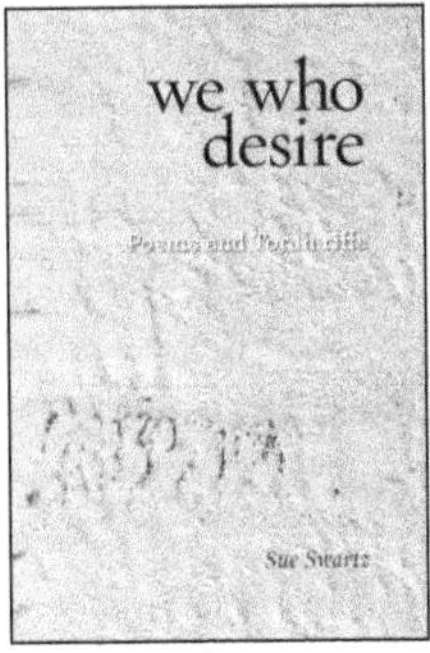

we who desire:
Poems and Torah riffs by Sue Swartz

"Sue Swartz does magnificent acrobatics with the Torah. She
takes the English that's become staid and boring, and adds
something that's new and strange and exciting. These are poems
that leave a taste in your mouth, and you walk away from them
thinking, what did I just read? Oh, yeah. It's the Bible."
—Matthue Roth, author of *Yom Kippur A Go-Go*

Open My Lips: Prayers and Poems
by Rachel Barenblat

"Barenblat's God is a personal God—one who lets her cry on His shoulder, and who rocks her like a colicky baby. These poems bridge the gap between the ineffable and the human. This collection will bring comfort to those with a religion of their own, as well as those seeking a relationship with some kind of higher power."
—Satya Robyn, author of *The Most Beautiful Thing*

Words for Blessing the World: Poems in Hebrew and English by Herbert J. Levine

"These writings express a profoundly earth-based theology in a language that is clear and comprehensible. These are works to study and learn from."
—Rodger Kamenetz, author of *The Jew in the Lotus*

Shiva Moon: Poems by Maxine Silverman

"The poems, deeply felt, are spare, spoken in a quiet but compelling voice, as if we were listening in to her inner life. This book is a precious record of the transformation saying Kaddish can bring."
—Howard Schwartz, author of *The Library of Dreams*

is: heretical Jewish blessings and poems by Yaakov Moshe (Jay Michaelson)

"Finally, Torah that speaks to and through the lives we are actually living: expanding the tent of holiness to embrace what has been cast out, elevating what has been kept down, advancing what has been held back, reveling in questions, revealing contradictions."
—Eden Pearlstein, aka eprhyme

Texts to the Holy: Poems
by Rachel Barenblat

"These poems are remarkable, radiating a love of God that is full bodied, innocent, raw, pulsating, hot, drunk. I can hardly fathom their faith but am grateful for the vistas they open. I will sit with them, and invite you to do the same."
—Merle Feld, author of *A Spiritual Life*

The Sabbath Bee: Love Songs to Shabbat
by Wilhelmina Gottschalk

"Torah, say our sages, has seventy faces. As these prose poems reveal, so too does Shabbat. Here we meet Shabbat as familiar housemate, as the child whose presence transforms a family, as a spreading tree, as an annoying friend who insists on being celebrated, as a woman, as a man, as a bee, as the ocean."
—Rachel Barenblat, author of *The Velveteen Rabbi's Haggadah*

All the Holes Line Up: Poems and Translations
by Zackary Sholem Berger

"Spare and precise, Berger's poems gaze unflinchingly at—but also celebrate—human imperfection in its many forms. And what a delight that Berger also includes in this collection a handful of his resonant translations of some of the great Yiddish poets." —Yehoshua November, author of *God's Optimism* and *Two World Exist*

How to Bless the New Moon:
Songs of the Sovereign and the Icon
by Rachel Kann

"Rachel Kann is a master wordsmith. Her poems are rich in content, packed with life's wisdom and imbued with soul. May this collection of her work enable more of the world to enjoy her offerings."
—Sarah Yehudit Schneider, author of *You Are What You Hate* and *Kabbalistic Writings on the Nature of Masculine and Feminine*

Into My Garden
by David Caplan

"The beauty of Caplan's book is that it is not polemical. It does not set out to win an argument or ask you whether you've put your tefillin on today. These gentle poems invite the reader into one person's profound, ambiguous religious experience."
— *The Jewish Review of Books*

Between the Mountain and the Land is the Lesson: Poetic Midrash on Sacred Community
by Abe Mezrich

"Abe Mezrich cuts straight back to the roots of the Midrashic tradition, sermonizing as a poet, rather than idealogue. Best of all, Abe knows how to ask questions and avoid the obvious answers."
—Jake Marmer, author of *Jazz Talmud*

NOKADDISH: Poems in the Void
by Hanoch Guy Kaner

"A subversive, midrashic play with meanings–specifically Jewish meanings, and then the reversal and negation of these meanings."
—Robert G. Margolis

An Added Soul: Poems for a New Old Religion
by Herbert J. Levine

"These poems are remarkable, radiating a love of God that is full bodied, innocent, raw, pulsating, hot, drunk. I can hardly fathom their faith but am grateful for the vistas they open. I will sit with them, and invite you to do the same."
—Merle Feld, author of *A Spiritual Life.*

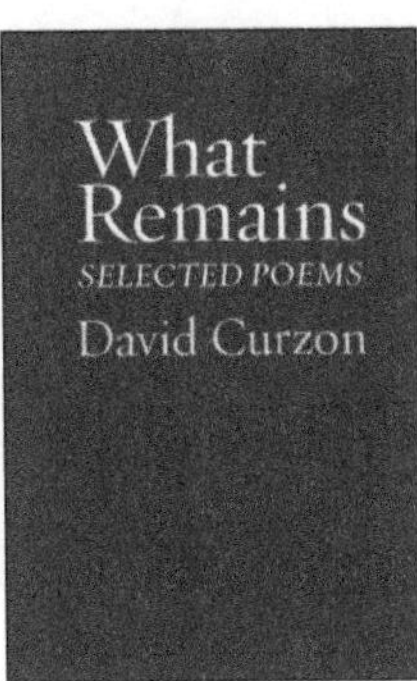

What Remains
by David Curzon

"Aphoristic, ekphrastic, and precise revelations animate WHAT REMAINS. In his stunning rewriting of Psalm 1 and other biblical passages, Curzon shows himself to be a fabricator, a collector, and an heir to the literature, arts, and wisdom traditions of the planet."
—Alicia Ostriker, author of *The Volcano and After*

The Shortest Skirt in Shul
by Sass Oron

"These poems exuberantly explore gender, Torah, the masks we wear, and the way our bodies (and the ways we wear them) at once threaten stable narratives, and offer the kind of liberation that saves our lives."
—Alicia Jo Rabins, author of *Divinity School*, composer of *Girls In Trouble*

Walking Triptychs
by Ilya Gutner

These are poems from when I walked about Shanghai and thought about the meaning of the Holocaust.

Book of Failed Salvation
by Julia Knobloch

"These beautiful poems express a tender longing for spiritual, physical, and emotional connection. They detail a life in movement—across distances, faith, love, and doubt."
—David Caplan, author of *Into My Garden*

Daily Blessings: Poems on Tractate Berakhot
by Hillel Broder

"Hillel Broder does not just write poetry about the Talmud; he also draws out the Talmud's poetry, finding lyricism amidst legality and re-setting the Talmud's rich images like precious gems in end-stopped lines of verse."
—Ilana Kurshan, author of *If All the Seas Were Ink*

The Missing Jew: Poems 1976-2022
by Rodger Kamenetz

"How does Rodger Kamenetz manage to have so singular a voice and at the same time precisely encapsulate the world view of an entire generation (also mine) of text-hungry American Jews born in the middle of the twentieth century?"
—Jacqueline Osherow, author of *Ultimatum from Paradise* and *My Lookalike at the Krishna Temple: Poems*

The Red Door: A dark fairy tale told in poems
by Shawn C. Harris

"THE RED DOOR, like its poet author Shawn C. Harris, transcends genres and identities. It is an exploration in crossing worlds. It brings together poetry and story telling, imagery and life events, spirit and body, the real and the fantastic, Jewish past and Jewish present, to spin one tale."
—Einat Wilf, author of *The War of Return*

The Matter of Families
by Robert H. Deluty

"Robert Deluty's career-spanning collection of New and Selected poems captures the essence of his work: the power of love, joy, and connection, all tied together with the poet's glorious sense of humor. This book is Deluty's masterpiece."
—Richard M. Berlin, M.D., author of *Freud on My Couch*

The Five Books of Limericks
by Rhonda Rosenheck

"A biblical commentary that is truly unique. Each chapter of the Torah is distilled into its own limerick, leading the reader to reconsider the meaning of the original text, and opening avenues for interpretation that are both fun and insightful."
—Rabbi Hillel Norry

Bits and Pieces
by Edward Pomerantz

"A stunning tapestry of family life in the 40s and 50s. Like all great poetry, Pomerantz's work expands after reading. Each poem is exquisitely structured, often with a stunning ending, into a masterful whole."
—Alan Ziegler, editor of SHORT: *An International Anthology*

Words for a Dazzling Firmament: Poems/ Readings on Bereishit Through Shemot
by Abe Mezrich

"Mezrich is a cultivated craftsman— interpretively astute, sonically deliberate, and spiritually cunning."
—Zohar Atkins, author of *Nineveh*

Everything Thaws
by R. B. Lemberg

"Full of glacier-sharp truths, and moments revealed between words like bodies beneath melting permafrost. As it becomes increasingly plain how deeply our world is shaped by war and climate change and grief and anger, articulating that shape feels urgent and necessary and painful and healing."
—Ruthanna Emrys, author of *A Half-Built Garden*

Ode to the Dove
*An illustrated, bilingual edition of
a Yiddish poem by Abraham Sutzkever*
Zackary Sholem Berger, translator
Liora Ostroff, Illustrator

"An elegant volume for lovers of poetry."
—Justin Cammy, translator of *Sutzkever, From the Vilna Ghetto
to Nuremberg: Memoir and Testimony*

Poems for a Cartoon Mouse
by Andrew Burt

"Andrew Burt's poetry magnifies the vanishingly small line
between danger and safety. This collection asks whether order
is an illusion that veils chaos, or vice-versa, juxtaposing images
from the Bible with animated films."
—Ari Shapiro, host of NPR's *All Things Considered*

Old Shul
by Pinny Bulman

"Nostalgia gives way to a tender theology, a softly chuckling
illumination from within the heart of/as a beautiful, broken
sanctuary, somehow both gritty and fragile, grimy and
iridescent – not unlike faith itself."
—Jake Marmer, author of *Cosmic Diaspora*

Feet In L.A., But My Womb Lives In Jerusalem, My Breath In Vermont
by Lori Levy

"Reading through Lori Levy's new book of poems takes my
breath away. With no pretense whatsoever, they leap, alive, from
the page until this reader felt as if she were living Levy's life.
How does the author do it?"
—Mary Jo Balistreri, author of *Still*

Printed in the USA
CPSIA information can be obtained
at www.ICGtesting.com
CBHW021552250624
10644CB00005B/57